Animals Helping to Keep the Peace

TAMRA B. ORR

Children's Press®
An Imprint of Scholastic Inc.
New York Toronto London Auckland Sydney
Mexico City New Delhi Hong Kong
Danbury, Connecticut

Content Consultant
Dr. Stephen S. Ditchkoff
Professor of Wildlife Sciences
Auburn University
Auburn, Alabama

Library of Congress Cataloging-in-Publication Data
Orr, Tamra, author.
 Animals helping to keep the peace / by Tamra B. Orr.
    pages cm. — (A true book)
 Summary: "Learn how animals can be trained to work in law enforcement and military posi-
tions."— Provided by publisher.
 Audience: Ages 9–12.
 Audience: Grades 4 to 6.
 Includes bibliographical references and index.
 ISBN 978-0-531-21213-4 (library binding) — ISBN 978-0-531-21287-5 (pbk.)
 1. Animals—War use—Juvenile literature. 2. Animals in police work—Juvenile literature. 3.
Working animals—Juvenile literature. I. Title. II. Series: True book.
 UH87.O77 2015
 355.4'24—dc23   2014030573

© 2015 Scholastic Inc.
All rights reserved. Published in 2015 by Children's Press, an imprint of Scholastic Inc. Published
simultaneously in Canada. Printed in China 62
SCHOLASTIC, CHILDREN'S PRESS, A TRUE BOOK™, and associated logos are trademarks and/or
registered trademarks of Scholastic Inc.
2 3 4 5 6 7 8 9 10 R 24 23 22 21 20 19 18 17

Front cover: A military dog in training

**Back cover: A dog searching the
World Forum congress center in
The Hague, Netherlands**

Find the Truth!

Everything you are about to read is true *except* for one of the sentences on this page.

Which one is **TRUE**?

T or F Dogs are the best at helping the military keep the peace.

T or F Soldiers are still relying on animals to help them during battle.

Find the answers in this book.

3

Contents

THE **BIG** TRUTH!

Dogs are more than loving
pets, they can also be heroes!

Animals are helping keep things safe everywhere—including underwater.

Military dogs and their handlers are often best friends.

Gas attacks were common during World War I.

CHAPTER 1

Sergeant Stubby

The sergeant woke from a sound sleep. He lifted his head. He knew something was wrong, but what was it? He had been in the war for months. During that time, he had developed a reputation for protecting his men. A few months earlier, he had saved them from a surprise **mustard gas** attack. Thanks to his excellent sense of smell, he had noticed the gas before anyone else.

Mustard gas got its name from its yellow color and unique smell.

Searching for Spies

This time, the sergeant did not smell anything. He heard something, and it sounded suspicious. He followed the noise and found a German spy. The enemy soldier was drawing a map of where the Americans were sleeping. Sergeant Stubby made a loud sound to warn the other men. Then he grabbed the spy and refused to let go until the rest of the men came to help.

Soldiers slept in bunk buildings called barracks.

J. Robert Conroy poses for a photo with Sergeant Stubby in 1919.

Minutes later, Private J. Robert Conroy came around the corner. He had woken up when Sergeant Stubby left the bunk. He knew his friend had good instincts for trouble, so he listened carefully. When he heard a gasp of pain, Conroy grabbed his rifle and came to investigate. He quickly found the sergeant and his newly captured prisoner. Conroy went right to work disarming the German.

Even though he was a dog, Stubby was an important part of his division.

An Unusual Hero

Convincing Sergeant Stubby to let go of the spy was not easy. He was determined to hold on as long as he could—with his teeth. Stubby was a little different than the other soldiers. He was much smaller, and he walked on four legs. He also barked warnings and used his teeth as a weapon. Sergeant Stubby was a pit bull and a member of the U.S. Army's 102nd Infantry Division.

Joining the Army

In the summer of 1917, the men of the 102nd Infantry were surprised to see a dog wander onto the training field in Connecticut. Before long, the soldiers had unofficially adopted him. Conroy took special care of the troop's new member. When orders came for the men to ship out to France, Conroy decided to take his four-legged friend with him. He smuggled the dog on board the transport ship that would carry them both to Europe.

The SS *Minnesota* carried Stubby and Conroy across the Atlantic Ocean to fight in World War I.

A Brave Companion

To the soldiers' surprise, their new pet was incredibly brave. He did not run when he heard **artillery** fire. He simply jumped into the **dugouts** with the men. Stubby often heard shells coming before the humans did, so the troops followed when he jumped into a hole. When Stubby smelled gas with his sensitive nose, he warned the men by barking and growling.

Soldiers relied on trenches and dugouts for protection during the war.

Stubby wore his medals on a special jacket.

Stubby was named for his extremely short tail.

For 18 months, Sergeant Stubby did his best to protect the men. When soldiers were hurt, he tracked them down and barked until **medics** arrived. Stubby was injured a few times during his adventures. However, the soldiers made sure he received excellent medical care. He was always able to get right back in the battle. No one knows how many lives Stubby saved, but he was truly a hero.

Stubby died on March 16, 1926, in the arms of J. Robert Conroy.

Stubby rides on a float during a parade in 1921.

A Returning Hero

Stories of Sergeant Stubby's adventures were published in newspapers throughout the United States. When World War I (1914–1918) ended, the dog came home a well-known and beloved hero. He led city parades and was made an honorary member of such groups as the American Red Cross and the American Legion. Stubby toured the country and even met several presidents.

America's First War Dog

Sergeant Stubby was the nation's first military dog. From the first time he warned soldiers of trouble to the last time a medal was pinned on his military vest, he showed the world why dogs have been considered "man's best friend" for so long. For the next several decades, dogs proved themselves on the battlefield over and over.

A war dog jumps over a trench on its way to deliver a message.

A military dog and his fellow soldiers patrol near a road in Afghanistan.

CHAPTER 2

On the Ground

Ever since Sergeant Stubby, dogs have been an important part of the military. They have served on the battlefields of World War I, World War II (1939–1945), and the Vietnam War (1954–1975). They have also helped fight in the Persian Gulf and Afghanistan. Dogs are helpful in war for many of the same reasons they make such wonderful pets. They are very loyal to their owners. They are also easy to train and can quickly learn to follow commands.

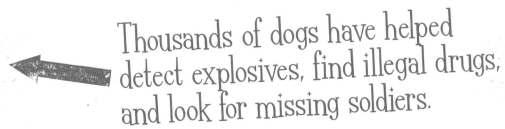

Thousands of dogs have helped detect explosives, find illegal drugs, and look for missing soldiers.

Superb Senses

Dogs' skills go beyond being friendly and obedient. A dog's brain is different than a human's. A larger part of it is dedicated to the senses of sight and smell. This means dogs can see and smell different things than humans can. A dog's nose also has many more **receptors** than a human's. This helps the dog smell even the faintest odors. Finally, dogs can see very well in the dark.

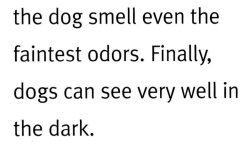

Dogs can learn to identify thousands of different chemicals by their smell.

A dog delivers medical supplies to the front lines during World War I.

Many Jobs to Do

Military dogs are trained in many skills. Most are single-purpose dogs. This means they are trained for a specific job. Some are taught to locate mines, rescue wounded soldiers, or deliver messages. Others are taught to search silently for spies or **snipers** and defeat enemies without using **lethal** force. Because most dogs are small enough to fit into tight spaces, they are sometimes trained to investigate tunnels where people cannot fit.

Dogs were used to explore enemy tunnels during the Vietnam War.

World War II

During World War II, thousands of dogs worked for the armed forces. Some were **sentries**. They were responsible for patrolling and guarding supplies or facilities. In 1943, more than 3,000 sentry dogs patrolled beaches for signs of enemy boats or submarines. Other dogs were scouts. They were trained to detect enemy soldiers. If a scout dog sensed a nearby foe, it froze in place, pricked up its ears, and stiffened its tail until a human soldier arrived to investigate.

Today's Top Dogs

All branches of the armed forces use military dogs. The marines use them to sniff out bombs and the people who plant them. The dogs wear radios on their backs so they can hear commands from far away. Special-ops troops parachute out of planes or **rappel** over mountainsides alongside their dogs. These dogs are equipped with high-tech equipment such as heat-sensing cameras and waterproof vests.

Trained dogs can join their handlers in sliding down ropes out of helicopters.

Tiny Triumph

Although most military dogs are fairly big breeds, Smoky was an exception. A Yorkshire terrier, she weighed just 4 pounds (1.8 kilograms) and stood 7 inches (17.8 centimeters) tall. During World War II, Smoky rode in soldiers' bags. She went along on many air and sea rescue missions and survived 150 air raids. She also entertained wounded soldiers. After the war, Smoky visited veterans in hospitals to cheer them up and make them smile.

Police dogs can find explosives, drugs, or other illegal items.

Experts believe that each military dog saves the lives of around 150 soldiers on average.

Saving Lives

There are more than 2,700 dogs serving in the military today. Around 600 of them are in active war zones. In addition to the military, the Central Intelligence Agency (CIA) and local police forces also use dogs to help protect people. These dogs are trained to detect explosives, take down criminals, and search for suspects.

THE **BIG** TRUTH!

The Right Breeds

When the U.S. military first began using dogs, it used a variety of breeds. However, it began to be noticed over time that some breeds were much better than others at performing military jobs. Eventually, military leaders narrowed their list of working breeds to five, shown here. These dogs are known for being smart, loyal, strong, and easy to train.

German Shepherds

Giant Schnauzers

Farm Collies

Belgian
Sheepdogs

Doberman
Pinschers

A bottlenose dolphin leaps during a training session in the Persian Gulf. The dolphin will help clear the water of mines.

CHAPTER 3

In the Sea and Air

Dogs have helped save the lives of countless soldiers, but they are not the only animals to help people. A number of other animals have lent their paws, wings, and flippers to help the armed forces over the last century. These heroic species include bottlenose dolphins, beluga whales, California sea lions, and pigeons.

A device on the dolphin's fin allows its handler to track the dolphin's location underwater.

In the Air

Carrier pigeons are birds that have two unique abilities. First, they have an internal **compass** that helps them navigate from one place to the next—and remember the route. Second, they are easily trained to fly to a specific location and back again. These two skills have kept carrier pigeons delivering messages and documents since at least 1870.

Training a carrier pigeon takes only around eight weeks.

Messages are attached to a carrier pigeon's legs.

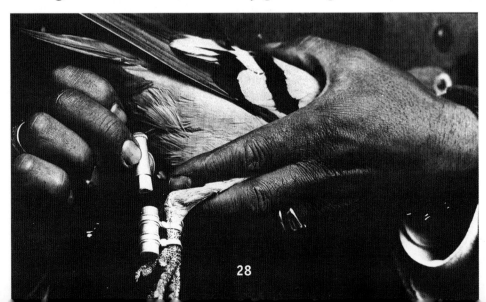

British soldiers send a carrier pigeon on a mission during World War II.

During World Wars I and II, more than 54,000 carrier pigeons delivered maps, reports, and government messages. These pigeons were very fast. Flying at speeds of up to 60 miles (97 kilometers) per hour, they often covered 200 to 600 miles (322 to 966 km) per flight. Documents were placed inside small tubes attached to the birds' legs or in larger capsules on their backs. Some pigeons even carried cameras that took photos of enemy targets.

A replica of Cher Ami is on display at the International Spy Museum in Washington, D.C.

The name *Cher Ami* is French for "dear friend."

A Legendary Pigeon

One of the most famous carrier pigeons in history was Cher Ami. This bird flew on 12 missions during World War I. He once saved an entire troop from certain death by getting a cease-fire message to the right place in time. When the famous bird finally died in 1919, his remains were put on display at Washington's Smithsonian Institution.

In the Water

Trained sea lions, dolphins, and beluga whales are used to patrol the water. Starting in 1960, the U.S. Navy began training these species to deliver equipment to divers and to find lost people. They can also recover military equipment and even guard American submarines by watching for enemy swimmers. Some of the animals carry cameras in their mouths to take photos.

U.S. Navy marine mammal experts train a sea lion.

31

Searching the Seas

Dolphins navigate through the water using **echolocation**. They create mental maps of their environment using the information they receive from sound waves bouncing back at them. The navy trained hundreds of underwater creatures to use their echolocation for important jobs during the Vietnam War and the Persian Gulf War.

Other animals like bats use echolocation to navigate during the night.

Dolphins emit special sound waves that bounce off objects and return to the animal.

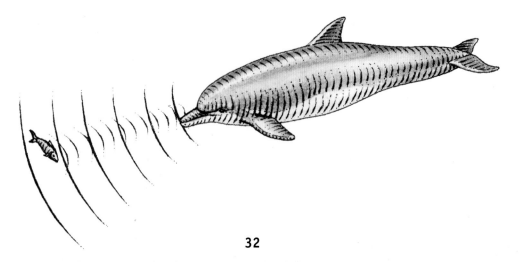

A sea lion gets ready to attach a reel line to an object on the sea floor during a training exercise.

Whales, dolphins, and sea lions were taught to locate underwater mines. Dolphins dropped a weight next to each mine so divers could find it. Sea lions attached rubber devices to the mines so they could be reeled in. Dolphins also swam around navy ships to look out for enemy swimmers who might try to plant bombs.

Like dogs, rats have an incredibly powerful sense of smell.

Rodents to the Rescue

The newest animal to join the military lineup is the rat. Rats might seem more like pests than helpful assistants. However, these rodents are being trained to use their sensitive noses to find abandoned land mines. Because they can resist most diseases, rats can go into areas that are too dangerous for people or dogs. In addition, they cost far less to train than dogs.

Feline Spies

A few other animals have been considered for military work. But most have not worked out as planned. For example, in the early 1960s, the CIA hoped to train cats to be spies. Operation Acoustic Kitty was based on surgically implanting microphone recorders into house cats. After multiple surgeries, the first cat was ready for its mission. However, it was almost immediately killed by a passing car. Operation Acoustic Kitty was over!

Cats have not been very useful for military or law enforcement jobs so far.

Military dogs often form close bonds with their handlers.

CHAPTER 4

When Military Animals Retire

Military animals are often seen as friends, partners, and fellow soldiers by the troops they serve with. The humans know they can depend on their animals to keep them safe, whether they are on the ground, in the air, or underwater. But what happens to these animals when the weapons are quiet and the war is over? Unfortunately, this is a complicated question that people are still trying to answer.

 Many military dogs are adopted by loving families after the battles are over.

A Sad Ending

During the Vietnam War, thousands of war dogs fought side by side with soldiers. When the U.S. military left Vietnam and the soldiers went home in 1973, most of the dogs were left behind and **euthanized**. Why? At that time, the dogs were thought of as equipment, just like a tank or a weapon. No effort was made to get them back home.

Timeline of Military Service

1917

Sergeant Stubby becomes the first military dog in the United States.

1956

The nation's carrier pigeon program is shut down by the U.S. Army.

More Than Equipment

While the army classified the dogs as equipment, their handlers thought differently. "A handler would never speak of their dog as a piece of equipment," stated Gerry Proctor, a spokesman for the Lackland Air Force Base in Texas, where military dogs are trained. "The dog is their partner. You can walk away from a damaged tank, but not your dog. Never."

1964–1973
Approximately 5,000 dogs fight in the Vietnam War.

2013
President Barack Obama signs a law that ensures all retired military dogs are properly cared for.

Deserving Our Respect

In recent years, many people have been pushing to change the status of military dogs from "equipment" to "soldier dogs" or "canine members of the armed forces." This would give the animals the respect they deserve. This idea gained support after a military dog named Cairo helped in the 2011 mission to capture terrorist leader Osama bin Laden. Since then, the number of people who want to adopt retired military dogs has soared.

The Dickin Medal is an award given to war animals. Past recipients include carrier pigeon G.I. Joe, Rob the war dog, and Warrior, a war horse.

Dogs work just as hard as human soldiers, and they deserve to be treated respectfully.

Dogs go through careful training programs at Lackland Air Force Base.

A New Law

On January 2, 2013, President Barack Obama signed a new law that will help countless military dogs throughout the country. It allows the military to transfer all retired soldier dogs to Lackland Air Force Base or other locations. From there, the animals can be adopted by families who will care for them. The government pays the cost of flying the dogs back to the United States, as well as for any medical care the animals might need.

Cyborg Bugs?

What animals might keep people safe in the future?
Scientists are focusing on creating bees and wasps
with radio equipment smaller than a grain of rice
attached to their bodies. This equipment allows
the insects to be tracked. One day they might be
used to gather and send important information.
That caterpillar in the corner might be recording a
conversation—or using internal sensors to detect
chemical threats!

War Heroes

Soldiers from every military branch have been recognized for the bravery they show in the face of war. For decades, those soldiers have known how much military animals have helped them do their jobs. From detecting a hidden bomb to capturing an undercover spy to tagging a misplaced mine to patrolling a high-security supply shed, these heroic animals have risked their lives to do just what human soldiers do: keep the peace. ★

On October 28, 2013, a national monument to honor military dogs was unveiled at Lackland Air Force Base in San Antonio, Texas.

Dogs will continue to play an important role in military operations for many years to come.

Number of lives saved by war dogs throughout U.S. history, according to the U.S. War Dogs Association: 10,000

Number of lives saved by Vietnam War dog Duke when he warned his troops of an incoming ambush: 100

Number of war dogs currently in service around the world: Around 2,500

Number of war dogs currently serving overseas: Around 700

Average length of a military dog's career: 10 years

Number of U.S. Navy marine mammal teams: 5

Did you find the truth?

F Dogs are the best at helping the military keep the peace.

T Soldiers are still relying on animals to help them during battle.

Resources

Books

Albright, Rosie. *Military Dolphins*. New York: PowerKids Press, 2012.

Bausum, Ann. *Stubby the War Dog: The True Story of World War I's Bravest Dog*. Washington, D.C.: National Geographic, 2014.

Dunn, Joeming. *Cher Ami: WWI Homing Pigeon*. Edina, MN: Magic Wagon, 2012.

Ruffin, Frances E. *Military Dogs*. New York: Bearport Publishing, 2007.

Storey, Neil. *Animals in the First World War*. Oxford, NY: Shire Publications, 2014.

Visit this Scholastic Web site for more information on animals helping to keep the peace:

★ www.factsfornow.scholastic.com

Enter the keywords **Animals Helping to Keep the Peace**

Important Words

artillery (ahr-TIL-ur-ee) — large, powerful guns that are mounted on wheels or tracks

compass (KUHM-pass) — an instrument with a magnetic pointer that always points north, used for finding directions

dugouts (DUHG-outz) — rough shelters dug out of the ground or in the side of a hill

echolocation (eh-koh-loh-KAY-shuhn) — the process of using sound waves to locate the position of objects in the air or water

euthanized (YOO-thuh-nyzed) — killed painlessly

lethal (LEE-thuhl) — deadly

medics (MED-iks) — people who are trained to give medical treatment in an emergency or in the military

mustard gas (MUHS-turd GAS) — a deadly chemical gas that damages the lungs

rappel (ruh-PEL) — move down a steep incline or an overhang using a rope

receptors (ruh-SEP-turz) — sensory nerves

sentries (SEN-treez) — people who stand guard and warn others of danger

snipers (SNI-purz) — people who shoot from hidden places

Index

Page numbers in **bold** indicate illustrations.

About the Author

Tamra Orr is the author of hundreds of books for readers of all ages. She has a degree in English and secondary education from Ball State University, and now lives in the Pacific Northwest. She is the mother of four children, and loves to spend her free time reading, writing, and going camping. She has had birds, fish, cats, and dogs as pets and was amazed to see how these different animals could be used to help soldiers. She can rarely get her dog to come when she calls it!